CONTINENTS
OF THE WORLD

EUROPE

David Flint

First published in 2005 by Hodder Wayland,
an imprint of Hodder Children's Books

© Hodder Wayland 2005

Commissioning editor: Victoria Brooker
Editor: Kelly Davis
Inside design: Jane Hawkins
Cover design: Hodder Wayland
Series concept and project management by
EASI-Educational Resourcing
(info@easi-er.co.uk) Statistical research: Anna Bowden

Population Distribution Map
© 2003 UT-Battelle, LLC. All rights reserved.
Data for population distribution maps reproduced under licence from UT-Battelle, LLC.
All rights reserved.

Maps and graphs: Martin Darlison, Encompass Graphics

British Library Cataloguing in Publication Data

Flint, David
 Europe. – (Continents of the world)
 1. Europe – Juvenile literature
 I.Title
 970

ISBN 0 750246782

Printed and bound in China

Hodder Children's Books
A division of Hodder Headline Limited
338 Euston Road, London NW1 3BH

Picture acknowledgements
The author and publisher would like to thank the following for allowing their
pictures to be reproduced in this publication:
Corbis 1 (Chris Lisle), 5 (Catherine Karnow), 6 (Michael T. Sedam), 11 (Bettmann), 13 (David Turnley),
14 (ML Sinibaldi), 17 (Chris Rainier), 18 (Daniel Lainé), 22 (Michel Setboun), 24 (Reuters/Fabrizio
Bensch), 25(t) (Howard Davies), 25(b) (Les Stone), 26 (Reuters/Pablo Sanchez), 27 (Peter Turnley), 28
(Reuters/Vincenzo Pinto), 29 (David Rubinger), 30 (Tomo Ikic), 31 (Kai Pfaffenbach), 32 (© National
Gallery Collection, 1838), 33 (Laszlo Veres/B.D.V), 35 (Michael St Maur Sheil), 36 and 44 (Adam
Woolfitt), 38 (Tony Aruzza), 39 (Ian Beames), 43 (Marco Cristofori), 45 (Ed Kashi), 46 (Barry Lewis), 47
(Reuters/Vincent Kessler), 48 (Enzo and Paolo Ragazzini), 49 (Louise Gubb), 50, 52 and 54 (Reuters),
51 (Architecture Studio/Vincent Kessler), 53 (Fabian Cevallos), 56 (Jonathan Blair), 59(t) Fatih Saribas,
59(b) (Reuters/John Schults); EASI-Images 20, cover inset and 40, 41, 55 and 57 (Rob Bowden), main
cover (Roy Machonachie); Mary Evans Picture Library 7, 8, 9, 10 and 12; MRP Photography 34 (Martyn
Pitt); Edward Parker 3, 16, 19, 37, 42 and 58.

Cover picture: Brightly painted buildings line the Nyhavn Canal in the Danish capital of Copenhagen.
Once important for trade and industry, the Nyhavn region is now among the city's most popular tourist
attractions.

Rhine Gorge, near Bingen, Germany.

CONTENTS

EUROPE – A COMPLEX CONTINENT

Europe, including Russia, covers a total area of 23,758,441 square kilometres (9,173,134 square miles), and its 46 countries had a combined population of 1,003.5 million people in 2003. For hundreds of years, Europe led the world in many areas of human achievement, such as science, architecture and art. From the sixteenth century onwards, European powers, like Britain, Spain, France, Germany, Holland and Portugal, used their superior knowledge and scientific advances (in weaponry for example) to colonize large parts of Africa, Asia and South America.

In the twentieth century, Europe was the central arena for two world wars (1914-18 and 1939-45) that seriously weakened the countries of the region, draining their economies and costing millions of lives. In

Political divisions in Europe

Legend
★ Capital
• Major settlement

4

this weakened state, the political and economic dominance of European countries was overtaken by other nations, such as the United States and Japan. Nevertheless, Europe is still extremely important, partly because of its location at the heart of the northern hemisphere (the land between Asia and North America which contains the majority of the world's population). This central location gives Europe a powerful trading position and an important political role. Europe also still has strong trading, political, cultural and linguistic links with its former colonies in Africa, Asia, North America and South America.

THE EUROPEAN UNION

In 1957, six European countries (Belgium, France, West Germany, Italy, Luxembourg and the Netherlands) signed the Treaty of Rome. This treaty created the European Economic Community (EEC), an agreement that promoted free trade between member countries by abolishing or reducing import and export tariffs (taxes). The United Kingdom (UK), Denmark and the Irish Republic joined the EEC in 1974 and were joined by Greece in 1981, and Spain and Portugal in 1985. The EEC was renamed the European Union (EU) in 1992, when it became clear that its aims had expanded beyond free trade. The EU has since developed its own parliament to oversee issues of common interest to its member governments, such as security, social welfare and justice, environmental policy and regional and international development. In 2002, a common currency, called the euro, replaced the currencies of 12 member countries, and there are plans for other member states to adopt the euro in the future. In May 2004, the EU was expanded further to bring the total number of member countries to 25.

A pavement café in Paris, where people go to relax, socialize, and discuss art, politics and the issues of the day. 'Café culture' has been part of life in Europe for centuries.

1. THE HISTORY OF EUROPE

A MILLION YEARS AGO, THE FIRST HUMANS (CALLED *HOMO ERECTUS*) came from Africa to settle in southern Europe. Later, about 35,000 years ago, Cro-Magnon man, a more developed human ancestor skilled in tool-making and art and to which all modern humans are related, began to spread across Europe from Africa. From 4000 BC, these people lived in organized communities and were hunters and tool-makers during the Stone Age.

THE EARLY YEARS

In around 3000 BC, the Mediterranean island that we now call Crete emerged as the first state founded in Europe. Named the Minoan civilization after the legendary King Minos, its people made vases, statues and complex buildings.

The ruins of the Acropolis, the fortified citadel at the centre of ancient Athens.

Then, in the seventh century BC, Athens, located in modern-day Greece, developed as a powerful city-state at the centre of a growing Mediterranean empire. As its population grew, Athens expanded, gaining colonies in Italy, Sicily, Egypt and Turkey, and establishing the first form of democratic government. Meanwhile, in the dense forests of northern and eastern Europe, tribal peoples were still living as hunter-gatherers.

The first great European empire, Rome, was founded in 753 BC and reached its height in AD 117 under Emperor Hadrian. For over a thousand years, Rome ruled large parts of the continent, stretching from Britain in the west to Germany in the east, from North Africa in the south to the Baltic countries in the north. In AD 306 , the Roman emperor, Constantine, made Christianity the official state religion and Christianity spread rapidly. However, after AD 397, the Roman Empire was destroyed by invading Germanic tribes.

For two hundred years, beginning in the ninth century, the Vikings, warriors from Norway and Denmark, spread to much of western and southern Europe. At around the same time in eastern Europe, Russia grew as a small state centred on the city of Novgorod, until, in 1143, Moscow became Russia's nucleus.

THE MIDDLE AGES (ELEVENTH TO FOURTEENTH CENTURIES)

By the twelfth century, the feudal system had been established in Europe. Under the feudal system, the king gave land to the barons and bishops, who provided soldiers for the king's armies. Below the barons and bishops were the peasants. They worked on the land, and were protected by the barons and bishops. The twelfth and thirteenth centuries were a time of stability and population growth.

However, in the fourteenth century, Europe's population was dramatically reduced by famine (especially the great famine of 1316 when whole villages were abandoned), wars, such as the Hundred Years War (1337-1453), and the Black Death (bubonic plague). The Black Death was transmitted by fleas on rats, and killed one in three Europeans between 1347 and 1351. Because there were so many rats in Europe, and people lived in closely packed houses, the plague spread very rapidly. There were 73 million people in Europe in 1300 and only 45 million in 1400.

A 1665 engraving showing the devastation caused by the Black Death in Europe.

7

A Spanish treasure ship returns home, laden with gold and silver from South America.

RENAISSANCE AND EXPLORATION

The Renaissance, which started in Italy in about 1400 and then spread to the rest of Europe, was a revival of learning, science and culture when people began to re-examine the work of ancient Greeks and Romans. These works inspired artists such as Leonardo da Vinci and writers like Dante Alighieri.

The Renaissance movement in the arts was financed by profits from trade, and the growing enthusiasm for science helped to fuel interest in overseas exploration. During the fifteenth century, European explorers, such as Christopher Columbus (1451-1506), sailed to the Americas (then known as 'the New World') and Asia. These early explorers were looking for a new trade route to India and the Far East, and only encountered the New World by accident. As the century progressed, France, England and Holland began to control the exploration of the New World, as well as the trade and wealth derived from it.

By the seventeenth century, a triangular trade route had developed between Europe, Africa and the Americas. European goods were shipped to West Africa, where they were exchanged for slaves, who were transported to the West Indies. The ships then returned to Europe, carrying sugar, cotton and other West Indian goods.

RELIGION AND REVOLUTION

During the Middle Ages, the Roman Catholic Church had amassed enormous wealth and power in Europe. Then, in 1517, Martin Luther, a German monk, accused the Catholic Church of corruption, and attracted enough followers to create a divide within Christianity and establish the Protestant Church, which did not acknowledge the Pope's leadership. This religious split created a great deal of instability and conflict in Europe.

In contrast, the seventeenth century saw the rise of kings with absolute power who could use their armies to impose unity. Louis XIV, in France, was the most famous of these absolute rulers. At this time, the European nobility, who made up 5 per cent of the population, possessed great wealth and power, while the remaining 95 per cent of people had to endure poverty and hunger. Writers such as the Frenchman Jean-Jacques Rousseau (1712-78) questioned this state of affairs, and people began to discuss ideas of freedom and equality.

Disquiet among the masses culminated in the French Revolution of 1789. Louis XVI of France was executed in 1793, and France was transformed from a monarchy into a republic. Napoleon Bonaparte, a general in the Revolutionary armies, became so powerful that he overthrew the Revolutionary government. He then conquered much of Europe and crowned himself Emperor of France in 1804. However, after the defeat of his armies by the combined forces of Britain, Russia and Prussia, he was exiled. He later returned to Paris but was defeated in 1815, by the British and Prussian armies, after which Europe finally emerged as a series of independent countries.

For many years, poor French peasants had been paying a great deal of tax, while wealthy nobles and clergy paid very little tax. After a bad harvest in 1788, food was in short supply and the price of bread rose dramatically. King Louis XVI then increased his people's resentment by dismissing his popular finance minister, Jacques Necker, who had been trying to introduce reforms. On 14 July 1789, the common people rioted in Paris and stormed the Bastille (a famous prison), killing the governor and parading his head through the streets on a pike. This engraving shows the mob attacking the Bastille.

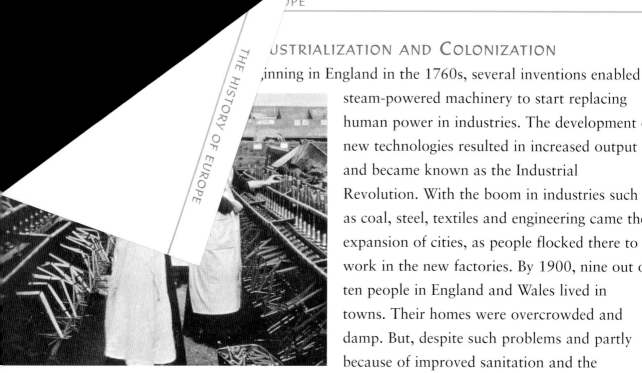

...USTRIALIZATION AND COLONIZATION

...inning in England in the 1760s, several inventions enabled steam-powered machinery to start replacing human power in industries. The development of new technologies resulted in increased output and became known as the Industrial Revolution. With the boom in industries such as coal, steel, textiles and engineering came the expansion of cities, as people flocked there to work in the new factories. By 1900, nine out of ten people in England and Wales lived in towns. Their homes were overcrowded and damp. But, despite such problems and partly because of improved sanitation and the provision of clean, safe drinking water, Europe's population grew from 190 million in 1800 to 420 million in 1900.

Machines like these increased the productivity of English textiles factories in the nineteenth century.

New methods of transport – first canals, and then railways – allowed rapid movement of people and goods. The Industrial Revolution helped Britain to become the richest country in the world and the new technology began to spread to the rest of Europe. Areas with large coal deposits developed new coalmines, together with many steel factories. Some of the most famous steel factories were at the town of Le Creusot in France and in the Ruhr area of Germany.

In 1800, Germany and Italy had consisted of groups of small states that were frequently in dispute with each other over local issues. During the nineteenth century, Germany and Italy began to emerge as powerful, united, industrialized countries. Meanwhile, richer

IN FOCUS:
Colonization

Spain, Portugal, Holland, Belgium, Britain, Germany and France all founded colonies in Africa, Asia and South America from the eighteenth century onwards, and there was great rivalry between these colonizing powers. By the early 1900s, Britain had the world's largest empire, including Canada, Australia, parts of the West Indies, and large areas of East Africa, South Africa and the Indian subcontinent.

European countries, such as Britain, France, Holland and Belgium, began to expand the colonies they had established earlier in Asia, Africa and the Americas.

Technological advances in agriculture were slower, but British ideas about stock-rearing and crop rotation to retain soil fertility gradually spread to the rest of Europe. The growth of industry also led to more efficient food production, enabling food supply to keep pace with rapid population growth.

WAR... AND PEACE

In the early twentieth century, Europe was devastated by the First World War (1914-18) – between the Central Powers (Germany, Austria-Hungary and Italy) and an alliance made up of Britain, France, Russia and the USA. Germany's power had been increasing, and the Allied nations were determined to stop any further German expansion in Europe. Following the USA's entry into the war in 1917, the combined Allied forces defeated the Central Powers in 1918. Many Germans believed that they had lost the war because their own government had betrayed them. This created a sense of bitterness, providing fertile ground in which Adolf Hitler could later sow his ideas about national pride in the 1930s.

The Russian communist leader, Vladimir Ilyich Lenin (1870-1924), speaking at a mass meeting in a public square in Moscow in 1920.

In Russia, all power had rested with the ruling Czars for hundreds of years. Then, in 1917, there was a revolution and the Bolsheviks (a political party) set up their own communist government, led by Vladimir Ilyich Lenin. Although the Czar, Nicholas II, had abdicated, he and his family were executed in 1918. The communist regime founded the Soviet Union in 1922, and ruled oppressively until it was overthrown in 1991.

German troops enter Poland during the Second World War.

During the 1920s and 1930s, nationalism (a movement to unify a nation) began to grow, aiding the rise of Adolf Hitler in Germany and Benito Mussolini in Italy. Hitler's Nazi Party persecuted ethnic minorities, especially the Jews, because the Nazis believed that the Jews were taking jobs from German people and that the German Aryan (or master) race was superior to any other race. In 1938, Germany took control of Austria and soon afterwards German troops invaded Czechoslovakia. The Second World War began in September 1939, when Hitler invaded Poland, and Britain and France declared war. By 1945, Germany, Italy and Japan had been defeated by the Allies (led by Britain and including the USA and the Soviet Union).

After the Second World War, much of Europe lay in ruins and the United States and the Soviet Union emerged as the two most powerful nations in the world. From 1945 onwards, during what became known as the 'Cold War', relations between the two powers were very strained as they competed for world leadership. Europe was now divided into two opposing areas, one in the West, dominated by the USA, which provided

IN FOCUS:
The Holocaust

During the Second World War (1939-45), hundreds of thousands of Jews were taken from German-occupied territories, such as Poland, France, Ukraine and the Netherlands, and transported to German labour camps. There, they were made to work as slave labourers and many died. In addition, more than two million Jews in German-occupied parts of the Soviet Union were murdered by German death squads, and over three million were sent to camps in Poland where they were gassed to death. The death camps were also used to kill millions of Jews from other countries in Europe. In total, over six million Jews were killed during the Second World War.

protection through NATO (the North Atlantic Treaty Organization), and one in the East, controlled by the Soviet Union and its allies, grouped in the Warsaw Pact. After the Second World War, western Europe prospered as a result of the Marshall Plan (about US$12 billion in aid provided by the USA). Meanwhile, the economy of eastern Europe stagnated.

In 1985, Mikhail Gorbachev became Soviet leader and introduced many liberal reforms. After a coup in 1991, Gorbachev was replaced by Boris Yeltsin, the Soviet Union was abolished and 15 new democratic states, including Russia and Ukraine, emerged. From 1992 onwards, former communist countries, such as Poland, Romania and Hungary, also started holding democratic elections, and communism in eastern Europe disintegrated.

In 1999, former communist allies Poland, Hungary and the Czech Republic joined NATO, and in 2004 ten more states joined the EU. By working together, all EU member countries benefit from increased trade. However, each member country also remains a sovereign nation, with its own view. For instance, the 2004 war with Iraq was supported by Britain and Spain but opposed by France and Germany.

The Berlin Wall was built in 1960, in order to stop refugees escaping from communist East Berlin to capitalist, democratic West Berlin. Its eventual demolition, in 1989, became a symbol of the fall of communism in eastern Europe. Here, jubilant protesters sit astride the Berlin Wall shortly before it was destroyed.

2. EUROPEAN ENVIRONMENTS

EUROPE IS AROUND 4,000 KM (2,480 MILES) LONG FROM NORTH TO south, extending northwards as far as the junction of the Arctic Ocean and the Atlantic Ocean and including Iceland. In the south, the Mediterranean Sea separates Europe and Africa. From east to west, Europe stretches some 5,500 km (3,417 miles), its western limits defined by the Atlantic Ocean and its eastern boundary with Asia outlined by the Ural mountains in Russia.

The Matterhorn, above the town of Zermatt in Switzerland, is one of the most beautiful and easily recognized peaks in the Alps.

MASSIVE MOUNTAINS

Europe's physical geography varies considerably, including vast forests, isolated wetlands, enormous plains, narrow river valleys, sandy islands and icy mountains. The Alps are the highest mountains in Europe and form a barrier between northern Italy and France and between Germany and Austria. Created by movements in the Earth's crust, the Alps have majestic, snow-covered, peaks, such as the Matterhorn (on the Swiss–Italian border); high-altitude lakes; and deep U-shaped valleys, some of which contain glaciers dating back to the last ice age – around 70,000 years ago.

Other mountainous areas, such as the Scottish highlands, are older, lower and less jagged because they have been worn down over millions of years. Europe also has some extensive lowland areas, such as the Netherlands, the Hungarian Plain and the valley of the River Po in Italy. These were all formed by the deposition of sand, silt and mud by large rivers.

The topography of Europe

Legend
▲ Mountain

VOLCANOES AND EARTHQUAKES

Europe has numerous active volcanoes, particularly in
Iceland and southern Italy. These are places where the
Earth's crust is thin and molten rock occasionally erupts
through a weak point to form a volcano. In time, the molten
rock cools and breaks down to form highly fertile soil.
Because of the soil's fertility, many people continue to farm
the land around volcanoes such as Mount Etna in Italy,
despite the danger of an eruption. Earthquakes also strike
parts of Europe in places where the Earth's crust is unstable.
Southern Greece and Turkey are particularly prone to
earthquakes, but minor earth tremors (often too small to
feel) occur in many parts of the continent.

FACT FILE

In 1999, an
earthquake in Turkey
killed 17,000 people
and injured 50,000.
Worse still was a
Turkish earthquake in
1939, which killed
33,000 people and left
over 700,000 homeless.

15

FACT FILE

About 27 per cent of the land in the Netherlands is below sea level and so has to be protected from the sea by dykes (earth embankments) and sea walls.

FACT FILE

The longest river in Europe is the Volga, which flows through Russia into the Caspian Sea. It is 3,685 km (2,290 miles) long.

The River Rhine has carved out a gorge here, near Bingen, in Germany.

SEAS, RIVERS AND LAKES

The Mediterranean Sea is important to Europe because it was one of the earliest routes between countries in the region. Except for the narrow Strait of Gibraltar between Spain and Morocco, the Mediterranean is virtually cut off from the Atlantic Ocean and so has no tides. Another European sea, the Baltic, is enclosed by Sweden, Finland, Germany and Denmark. However, the Baltic is much shallower than the Mediterranean and freezes for three months of the year, and therefore gets less shipping traffic. Europeans used to sail across the Atlantic Ocean to colonize other parts of the world and it remains an important trade route. Fishing is still important in the Atlantic, despite falling catches (caused by overfishing). The North Sea has the busiest shipping lanes in the world – in the Straits of Dover between Britain and France. The North Sea is also important for fish and for oil and gas, which are brought ashore in Britain and Norway.

Some of the largest rivers in Europe have their sources in the Alps. The Rhine (which runs through Switzerland, West Germany and the Netherlands), the Rhône (which runs through Switzerland and France), the Danube (which runs through Austria and Romania) and the Po (in Italy) all flow from the Alpine mountains down to the sea. Rivers like the Rhine have helped shape the landscape of Europe by carrying gravel, sand and mud sediments down from the mountains and depositing them in huge sheets on lower ground. As a result, countries like the Netherlands are partly composed of these sediments.

Europe has a number of lakes, many of which, like Lake Geneva in Switzerland, occupy valleys that were scoured out by glaciers thousands of years ago. Other lakes, like those along the River Don in Russia and the River Dnieper in the Ukraine, were created by dams constructed to help develop water resources for irrigation and to generate hydro-electric power (HEP). HEP uses the force of falling water to turn turbines that generate electricity.

PENINSULAS AND ISLANDS

Europe also has many peninsulas, such as Italy and Greece, both of which stick out into the Mediterranean Sea. Many of Europe's peninsulas are surrounded by lots of small islands. For example, Greece is composed of thousands of islands of varying sizes in the Aegean and Ionian Seas (part of the Mediterranean).

Further north, Denmark is made up of the Jutland Peninsula and the nearby islands in the Baltic and North Sea; while the Lofoten Islands in Norway are the most northerly inhabited islands. Sweden also has hundreds of islands off its coastline and the capital city, Stockholm, is actually spread across several of these islands. The British Isles is made up of two big islands (Great Britain and Ireland) and many smaller ones.

CLIMATE

Much of Europe has a mild, temperate climate, because the North Atlantic Drift (a northern extension of the Gulf Stream ocean current) carries warm, tropical water northwards along the west coast of Europe. By warming the air, the North Atlantic Drift also helps to protect much of western Europe from very cold winters. Europe is situated at a point

Many small fishing villages in northern Norway are built next to fiords (long, narrow, steep-sided coastal inlets). These fiords were carved out by glaciers during the last ice age and were then submerged when the sea level rose.

Russian winters are so cold that steel can snap and rivers freeze. Even the surface of the sea around St Petersburg has been known to freeze solid enough for vehicles to drive on it.

The River Neva freezes in the Russian city of St Petersburg.

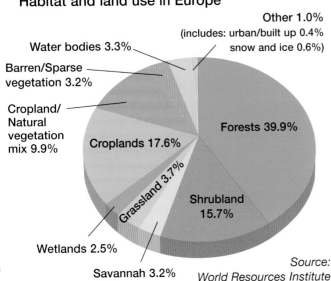

where cold, dry, polar air meets warm, moist, tropical air, creating an area of low barometric pressure (known as a depression) that is associated with cloud and rain, particularly in northern and western Europe.

There are three main types of climate in Europe. In the west, including the UK and Ireland, is the maritime climate, with fairly cool summers, mild winters and frequent light showers. Frost and snow are rare except in Scandinavia and Germany. Further east, countries like Austria and Russia have a continental climate, with long, very cold, dry winters. Snow covers the land for long periods, there are widespread frosts and some rivers freeze over. Summers here are short but hot, with frequent storms and showers. To the south is the Mediterranean climate, enjoyed by countries like Spain, southern France, and Italy, which have hot, dry summers, lots of sunshine and mild, wet winters.

Habitat and land use in Europe

- Other 1.0% (includes: urban/built up 0.4% snow and ice 0.6%)
- Water bodies 3.3%
- Barren/Sparse vegetation 3.2%
- Cropland/Natural vegetation mix 9.9%
- Croplands 17.6%
- Grassland 3.7%
- Forests 39.9%
- Shrubland 15.7%
- Wetlands 2.5%
- Savannah 3.2%

Source: World Resources Institute

NATURAL ENVIRONMENTS

In northern Europe there is a narrow belt of Arctic tundra with mosses and lichens but no trees. Temperatures can remain below freezing for up to ten months and a layer of permafrost (permanently frozen soil) lies beneath much of the surface. Plant growth is very slow and only a few animals have adapted to life in this harsh environment.

Further south is a region of marshy land and coniferous forests of pine, fir and spruce (known as taiga) that dominate large areas of Russia and Finland. Russia's taiga forests, which extend eastwards into Asia, form the largest continuous area of forest in the world. To the south and west of the taiga is an area of mixed forest that includes oak, chestnut and beech trees.

Further south still are grassy plains in Russia and the Ukraine, known as steppes. These plains have some of the most fertile soils in the world and so most of them have been turned into agricultural land.

Mediterranean areas, from Spain and Portugal in the west to Turkey in the east, often experience prolonged periods of dry weather. Grass cover is therefore often minimal, with heather and other drought-resistant shrubs and plants being more common. Pine and olive trees grow well in these conditions. And to the north of this region, where rainfall is more regular, vines grow well, making southern Europe one of the world's major wine-producing regions.

Italy's warm Mediterranean climate is ideal for growing grapes. These vineyards are in Piedmont, northern Italy.

● ● ● ● ● ● ● ➤ IN FOCUS: Mediterranean winds

Local winds affect many aspects of life in the Mediterranean. In spring, cold north winds blow down from the Alps towards the Mediterranean. In France this wind is called the Mistral and it blows down the Rhône valley at speeds of up to 130 km (81 miles) per hour. Farmhouses here are built without doors or windows on their northern sides to prevent the chilly northern winds getting in. In addition, rows of poplar or cypress trees are planted to break the force of the wind. A similar cold, north wind, called the Bora, affects countries such as Italy and Slovenia which border the Adriatic region of the Mediterranean coast.

3. THE PEOPLE OF EUROPE

EUROPE'S POPULATION HAS RISEN DRAMATICALLY, FROM ABOUT 250 million in 1800 to over 1,000 million (including Russia and Turkey) in 2004. During the nineteenth and twentieth centuries, better nutrition and hygiene led to a sharp fall in death rates (from 40 per 1,000 to 8 per 1,000), while birth rates stayed high at about 25 per 1,000. These high birth rates led to a period of rapid population growth in the UK – later repeated in countries such as Italy, Greece and Spain.

YOUNG AND OLD

Since 1950, the average birth rate has fallen to about 7 per 1,000 and population growth in much of Europe has slowed down. The falling birth rate has been partly due to improved medical care, resulting in much lower rates of infant mortality. For this reason, people no longer need to have lots of children in order to ensure that some will survive their infancy. Other factors behind the falling birth rate include people's desire for higher living standards, the wider availability of contraception and the fact that many people are having children later in life. The birth rate first began to fall in the UK in the twentieth century. This trend then spread to Norway, Germany and Italy and, more recently, to Greece and Spain. In other places, such as Turkey, the birth rate has only just begun to fall.

With fewer children being born, and many people living much longer (because of improved living conditions and healthcare), much of Europe now has an ageing population. Average life expectancy at birth in Europe has risen from

British senior citizens enjoy the view on the seafront, in Blackpool, northern England. Other British seaside towns, such as Bournemouth and Eastbourne, are also popular with retired people and have rapidly expanding elderly populations.

47 years in the early nineteenth century to over 70 years in the twenty-first century. This increased lifespan has important implications for nations such as France, Germany and the UK. For example, one concern is how to pay for all the pensions and care that elderly people will need in the future. Some politicians and economists believe that inward migration from Asia, parts of Africa and the Middle East will be the solution, providing workers to maintain the economies of these European countries.

POPULATION DENSITY

Europe has an average population density of 34 people per sq km (87 per sq mile). However, they are not spread evenly over the continent. Some places, such as parts of the Netherlands and South-East England, have high densities of 200 people per sq km (518 per sq mile), while others, such as the Massif Central in France (32 per sq km or 84 per sq mile) or northern

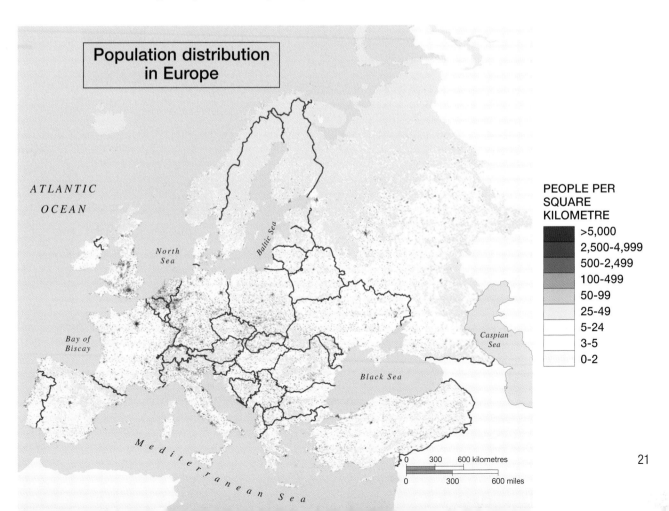

Population distribution in Europe

ATLANTIC OCEAN

North Sea

Baltic Sea

Bay of Biscay

Mediterranean Sea

Black Sea

Caspian Sea

PEOPLE PER SQUARE KILOMETRE

>5,000
2,500-4,999
500-2,499
100-499
50-99
25-49
5-24
3-5
0-2

0   300   600 kilometres

0   300   600 miles

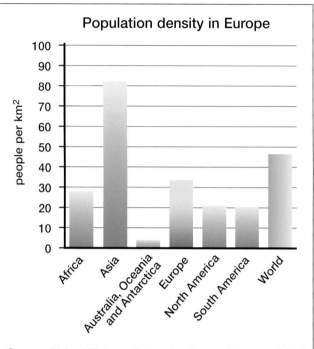

Population density in Europe

people per km²

(bar chart showing population density values for Africa, Asia, Australia, Oceania and Antarctica, Europe, North America, South America, and World, with a y-axis scaled from 0 to 100)

Source: United Nations; Britannica Book of the Year 2004

Norway (9 per sq km or 24 per sq mile) have much lower densities and so seem quite sparsely populated.

A high population density arc stretches across Europe, from South-East England, via the Netherlands, through the Rhine valley, to the valley of the River Po in Italy. This arc includes many large cities, such as Rotterdam in the Netherlands, Frankfurt in Germany and Milan in Italy. It also contains regions with access to a range of natural resources, such as the Ruhr in Germany (which is famous for its iron and steel). Other high population density areas include fertile farmland, such as the Paris basin (the area drained by the River Seine and its tributaries) in France. Ports, like Marseilles in France, or trading centres, such as Minsk in Belarus and London in the UK, also have high population densities.

Places with low population densities are often mountainous areas, such as the Alps or the Pyrenees (between France and Spain). Here, problems of steep terrain, high altitude and wet weather make for unsuccessful farming and there are few other resources, so it is very difficult for people to earn a living. Other sparsely populated places include those close to the Arctic Ocean where the climatic conditions test the limits of human endurance. However, not all cold areas have very low population densities. For example, Siberia in Russia is very cold for most of the year but, because it is rich in resources such as oil, gas, timber and minerals, some parts have become densely populated.

Two Saami people set out across the snow with their belongings bundled onto their sled in the sparsely populated region of Lapland, which includes parts of Finland, Norway, Sweden and Russia.

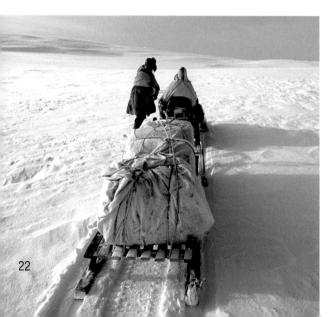

Capital cities, such as Rome, London, Moscow and Istanbul, have large numbers of people who are attracted by the industries and services based there. These capitals are not only manufacturing centres but also important financial, commercial and cultural centres.

MOVING WITHIN COUNTRIES

In the nineteenth and twentieth centuries, towns in Europe grew rapidly, as people migrated from the countryside in search of better-paid jobs in the factories. For example, in the UK in 1801 there was only one city (London) with over 100,000 people; by 1901 there were 33. There was a similar movement, from rural areas to towns and cities, in France, Germany and Russia, and sixty years later in Italy, Spain, Turkey and Greece.

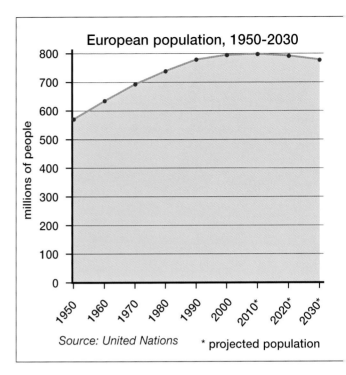

European population, 1950-2030

Source: United Nations   * projected population

However, since the 1990s, the pattern of movement has been reversed in countries such as France, the UK and Germany. For example, between 1991 and 2001 the population of London declined by 8 per cent as people moved from the city to the countryside. This process is called counter-urbanization. Many people decide to move because of the negative aspects of life in big cities, such as pollution, crime, noise and the high cost of housing and transport. Improvements in telecommunications, especially the Internet, have also allowed many people to work far from the commercial centres that are traditionally located in major cities.

MOVING BETWEEN COUNTRIES

People also move between countries. For example, during the 1960s the British government encouraged people from former British colonies in the West Indies, India, Pakistan and

FACT FILE

In 2004, Russia had the largest population in Europe, with 143.2 million people, while Liechtenstein and Monaco each had only 0.03 million people.

23

Turkish women living in Germany, in Berlin's Kreuzberg district, where there is a large Turkish community.

Bangladesh to migrate to cities such as Birmingham, London and Blackburn. This is partly why about 5 per cent of the UK population is of African or Asian origin.

In a similar way, people from Turkey and the former Yugoslavia (now Serbia and Montenegro) left their homes and went to find work in countries like Germany and Switzerland from the 1970s to the 1990s. Some returned home, but others chose to stay even when there was less work. For instance, in 2004, there were about two million people of Turkish origin living in Germany, together with 715,00 people from the former Yugoslavia and 613,000 Italians. Most of these people had arrived as guest workers in the 1970s and stayed on to live in Germany.

In 2004, there were about 7.5 million foreign workers in Europe, with another 8 million dependants (children and/or partners). Although European governments are aware that they need more migrant workers in order to fill employment gaps, the arrival of migrants has caused tensions in some areas. In the UK, for example, there have been protests by local people who claimed that migrants were benefiting from jobs, housing, education and healthcare at the cost of British people who were unable to find work or affordable housing. However, as Europe's population continues to age, and its workforce continues to decline because of falling birth rates, it will need more migrants to staff factories, offices, schools, hospitals and other services in the future.

ETHNIC DIVERSITY

The movements of people in Europe, both permanent and temporary, have produced great ethnic diversity. For example, people migrated from Algeria and Morocco into France in the 1980s and 1990s, adding to the mix of population already

In the early twenty-first century, many people from eastern European countries, such as the former Yugoslavia (especially the states of Bosnia and Serbia), Romania and Bulgaria, travelled to France, Germany and the UK. Other asylum seekers came from places like Afghanistan and Iraq, having fled war and religious persecution. So great were the numbers seeking asylum and a new life in the UK that, in 2002, large transit camps had to be built on the French coast to hold them. By 2004, better systems had been introduced to screen people claiming asylum. Numbers were reduced and the camps were removed but there were still many people seeking asylum from ethnic persecution.

Afghan asylum seekers, hoping to enter the UK, wait at the Sangatte Red Cross Centre in Calais, France, in 2002.

there and creating a diverse, multi-ethnic community, especially in French cities such as Marseilles and Paris. Migrants bring their own customs, religions and languages. Although the newly arrived migrants may become fully engaged in the economy of their new city, they tend to live in communities where others share their values and customs, and so help to create distinctive areas within cities such as Birmingham in the UK. For example, 70 per cent of school pupils aged 14 or under in Frankfurt, Germany, have parents who are foreign workers. Local people have benefited from the introduction of new ideas, new foods

Migrants, from northern Africa, at a market in Marseilles, in southern France.

and new friends. However, there have sometimes been tensions between locals and migrants, especially when locals have been unfamiliar with the customs of the newcomers and city authorities have made little effort to ease integration.

People in Spain demonstrating to show their opposition to ETA bombing campaigns.

Besides external influences, there is also ethnic diversity within many European countries, such as the Welsh in the UK and the Basque people in Spain. These different groups have their own languages and cultures, which are quite distinct from those of the nations to which they belong. Some of these groups feel a strong sense of identity and want independence from the wider nation in which they live. In the case of the Basque people, who live in the north-western part of Spain, this desire for independence has led to violence, with a terrorist group of Basque separatists called ETA carrying out many bombing campaigns against the Spanish people.

In other cases, such as Slovenia in the former Yugoslavia, ethnic groups have succeeded in gaining their independence peacefully and establishing separate states. Similarly, the break-up of the former Soviet Union after 1991 led to independence for countries such as Latvia, Lithuania, Estonia and Moldova.

Other peaceful separations include the Czech Republic and Slovakia, which reached an amicable agreement to separate and

The area of former Yugoslavia is inhabited by different ethnic groups – the Serbians, the Croatians and the Bosnians. In 1991 the Serbians lived mainly in the east, with some Serbian communities in Croatia and Bosnia. Most Serbians belong to the Orthodox Christian faith, the Croatians are mainly Roman Catholic, and the Bosnians are mainly Muslim. Fighting broke out in 1991, when Croatia declared its independence from Serbia. In 1992 the bitter fighting spread to Bosnia, which also declared its independence. Many people were killed and many homes were destroyed as people were forced to move.

Thousands of Bosnian men were killed in massacres

and others were incarcerated in prison. Peace only came in 1995 as a result of the efforts of UN peacekeeping forces from the USA, Britain, France and Germany, together with attempts by former US President Bill Clinton to broker a peace in the region. In 2004 several former leaders, including Radovan Karadzic (a former Serbian leader in Bosnia), were tried on charges of crimes against humanity for their role in encouraging attacks on Muslims and other ethnic groups.

Elderly Serbian refugees leaving their homes in Banja Luka, Bosnia, in 1995.

form two states in 1996. However, some minorities are so small that they cannot establish an independent state. Despite this, they may still demand recognition of their own language and culture from the majority ethnic group. This recognition may take the form of using different languages on official signs, government documents or voting papers.

FACT FILE

There are about 500,000 Roma (formerly called Gypsies) in Spain. There are still many Roma in eastern and central Europe where they form significant minorities.

4. EUROPEAN CULTURE AND RELIGION

THE MANY INVASIONS AND MIGRATIONS THAT EUROPE HAS experienced over the centuries have given the continent great linguistic diversity. Most European languages can be categorized as Celtic, Germanic (Dutch, German and English), Latin or Romance (Italian, French and Spanish), Slavonic or Baltic. The main language used for business in Europe is still English, although German is also popular. In most European countries, children learn at least two languages – their own and English.

People crowd into St Peter's Square in the Vatican City, Rome, for a papal blessing.

DIFFERENT RELIGIONS

Around 57 per cent of Europeans are Christians, with the Protestant Church dominant in northern countries such as Sweden, Denmark and Britain, and the Roman Catholic Church dominant in southern countries such as Spain, Italy and France. The Orthodox Church tends to dominate in eastern regions, such as Greece and Russia. However, religion has become less important in northern Europe. (For example, congregations have shrunk by 60 per cent in the UK since 1966.) Protestant churches have tried to adapt to changing social attitudes by appointing women priests and gay clerics.

In countries like Spain, France and Italy, many of the big celebrations are centred around religious festivals, such as Easter or Christmas. The Roman Catholic Church encourages its members to send their children to Catholic schools, so all over Europe there are thousands of Catholic primary and secondary schools. However, the Roman Catholic Church is finding it hard to recruit priests. (In the UK, the number of men coming forward to be ordained has fallen by 62 per cent since the 1990s.)

Religious divisions have led to problems in some parts of Europe. For example, in Northern Ireland there has been a long struggle between the Protestant Unionists, who wished Northern Ireland to remain part of Britain, and the Catholic Republicans, who wanted the North to be part of a united Ireland. During 'The Troubles' (1968-1998), this conflict led to a great deal of violence, including bombings and shootings. In 1998 a peace agreement was signed and, although there is still some tension, Northern Ireland has been much more peaceful since then.

Islam is also an important faith in Europe, accounting for almost 12 per cent of the continent's population. Turkey and Bosnia are almost entirely Muslim and, because of immigration from North Africa, there are growing numbers of Muslims in countries like France and Spain.

Other religions, like Hinduism and Sikhism, are widespread throughout Europe, with communities mostly concentrated in big cities where immigrant populations have settled and brought their religion with them. Judaism is also an important religion in Europe, and synagogues can be found in

FACT FILE

The south of Germany is predominantly Catholic and the north is mainly Protestant.

FACT FILE

The importance of Islam in Bosnia dates back to its occupation by Turkish forces from 1328 to 1878.

Muslims worshipping at a mosque in Turkey.

Religions in Europe

Non-religious 4.7%

Other 26.5% (includes Hinduism 0.1% Judaism 0.2%)

Islam 11.6%

Christianity 57.2%

Source: Britannica Book of the Year 2004

many cities, from London and Leeds in the UK to Rome in Italy. The number of Jews in Europe has fallen since the Second World War. For example, in 1933 there were 530,000 Jews in Germany and in 2003 there were just 61,000. Many Jews died in the Holocaust and others left Europe to live in Israel or the USA. There are also many smaller religious groups, such as Buddhists, in European cities.

FACT FILE

The zither is a flat musical instrument with strings that are plucked. It is used in the folk music of Central Europe.

MUSICAL EUROPEANS

Europe has a very long musical tradition. For example, Austria was the home of Wolfgang Amadeus Mozart (1756-91), who wrote over 600 pieces of classical music, while Germany produced Ludwig van Beethoven (1770-1827), who composed some of the world's best-known symphonies. In the twentieth century, Europe continued to produce leading classical composers, such as Benjamin Britten (1913-76), from the UK.

More recently, there have been many European rock and pop successes, beginning in the 1960s with groups such as the Beatles and the Rolling Stones from England. Other European acts with worldwide appeal have included Abba from Sweden and U2 from Ireland. Besides rock and pop music, Europe maintains strong folk music traditions, particularly those relating to traditional forms of dance, such as flamenco in Spain. Irish folk music and dancing has enjoyed particular popularity since the early 1990s, with shows such as *Riverdance* touring the world.

U2 in concert in Anaheim, California, USA, in 2001.

SPORTING PROWESS

Sports of many kinds are important in Europe, but none more so than football (or soccer). Football was invented in the UK and the first football association was founded in London in 1863. Since then, football has spread throughout the world but has remained particularly popular in Europe. Football championships are held in Europe every four years, and the 2004 championship was won by Greece.

Greece is better known as the home of the Olympic Games than as a footballing nation. Athletics contests first took place at Olympia, in Greece, almost 2,800 years ago, but the modern Olympics date back to games held in Athens, Greece, in 1896. In 2004, the Olympics returned to Athens, giving Greece a chance to celebrate its sporting heritage.

Golf, sailing, tennis, rugby, cycling and skiing are popular European sports. There is also a strong emphasis on gymnastics in countries such as Germany, Romania and Russia, where governments subsidize tuition for talented children to enable them to develop their skills from an early age.

A Hungarian athlete competes in the discus event at the 2004 Olympics in Athens.

EUROPEAN FOODS

The European diet varies considerably. Southern Europeans eat a lot of fish, pasta, salad, fruit and olive oil, while people in northern Europe tend to eat more meat, bread and fried foods.

People in eastern parts of Europe, such as Romania and Belarus, have diets that are rich in starch from potatoes but low in protein from meat and fish. Some European dishes have become world-famous. For example, pizza began as a dish for peasants in Italy but is now eaten all over the world. And many wines – like claret and champagne, from France – also originated in Europe.

ART AND DESIGN

Europe's artistic heritage includes some of the great names of art history. For example, Michelangelo Buonarroti (1475-1564) became famous in Florence in 1504 when he carved his statue of David. Michelangelo is also known for many other works, including his painting of the ceiling of the Sistine Chapel in Rome.

Other European painters reflected changing artistic styles throughout the centuries. For example, in the seventeenth century the Dutch painter Rembrandt (1606-1669) worked on both landscapes and religious paintings. In the eighteenth century in England, J.M.W. Turner (1775-1851) expressed intense emotion through his paintings of subjects such as stormy seas. Later approaches to art have included impressionism (which focused on the impact of changing light on natural scenes) in the works of Claude Monet (1840-1926) and other French artists; cubism (which moved away from representing a subject and towards abstract art) as in the works of Spanish artist Pablo Picasso (1881-1973); and

'The Fighting Téméraire', one of J.M.W. Turner's most famous works, painted in 1838.

surrealism (introducing ideas about the subconscious mind into art) in the paintings of Salvador Dali (1904-1989). More recently, British artists Damien Hirst and Tracy Emin have won critical acclaim for their sometimes shocking sculptures and artworks.

Some of the best European design is shown in the architecture of the region. The Acropolis in Athens and the Colosseum in Rome are examples of early European architecture, which were followed by the beautiful Renaissance churches of Italy. Since the 1950s, European architects have continued to push the boundaries of design – in buildings such as the Pompidou Centre in Paris and the Guggenheim Museum in Bilbao, Spain.

Design also includes fashion and Europe is home to some world-famous fashion houses, like Gucci in Rome and Versace in Paris. European fashion designers like Armani and Christian Dior influence the clothes that are later mass-produced and sold in shops across the world. The cities of Paris in France, Milan and Rome in Italy, and London in the UK have emerged as key centres for modern design and fashion in Europe.

British model, Naomi Campbell, modelling for the Italian designer, Gianni Versace.

●●●●●●▶ IN FOCUS: European City of Culture

The idea of choosing a European City of Culture, to encourage greater knowledge of European culture, began in Greece in 1983. Originally, a city within the EU was selected to be European City of Culture for one year. Cities selected for the title have included Athens, Greece; Glasgow, Scotland; Dublin, Ireland; and Amsterdam in the Netherlands. During its year of honour, each City of Culture organizes events for young people as well as arts festivals. In 1999 the title was changed to Cultural Capital of Europe and was opened to countries that were not members of the EU. In 2004, Genoa, in Italy, and Lille, in France, shared the honour; Liverpool, England, has been chosen for 2006. Being a City of Culture brings increased investment, growing tourism and many redevelopment schemes.

5. NATURAL RESOURCES IN EUROPE

THREE FOSSIL FUELS, COAL, OIL AND NATURAL GAS, ACCOUNT for 82 per cent of the energy consumed in Europe, and about 91 per cent of Europe's energy is supplied by imported gas or oil.

COAL AND GAS

In the nineteenth century, coal was the fuel of the Industrial Revolution in Europe. Because the availability of coal attracted large-scale industries, many villages in coalfields in France, Belgium, the UK, Russia and Germany turned into industrial cities. Examples include the steel industry in Sheffield, UK, the engineering industry in Lille, France, and the iron and steel industry in Donetsk, Russia. Coalfields in Poland and the Czech Republic later followed a similar pattern of development. However, in the twentieth century the demand for coal fell when large users switched to other fuels. For instance, the railways in western Europe began to use electric and diesel locomotives instead of steam engines, while gas and electricity largely replaced coal for domestic use.

Inside a coalmine at Thoresby, UK. Modern coalmines like this one are highly automated, so far fewer miners are needed than in the past.

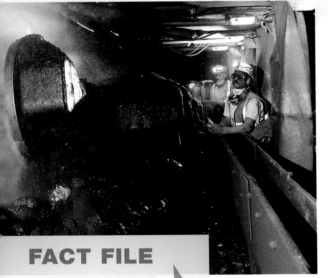

FACT FILE

Every year, about 101.6 million tons (100 million tonnes) of sulphur oxides are released into the Earth's atmosphere by burning coal. Europe is responsible for 18 per cent of these emissions.

Many coalfields all over western Europe have therefore closed down. The European Union (EU) has invested large sums of money in former coalfield areas in Germany, France and the UK, to help them develop new employment opportunities, but progress has been slow. Coalfields in Russia, Poland and the Czech Republic are still industrial centres but their supplies of coal are running out, and oil and gas are increasingly used in place of coal.

Natural gas has increased rapidly in importance over the last 20 years. A large gas field was discovered in the Netherlands in the 1950s, then more gas was found under the North Sea, and Norway and the UK became large gas producers. Russia also found very large deposits of oil and gas in Siberia and so became a major exporter, sending oil and gas to Germany, France, UK and Poland. Gas has become extremely important in western Europe, where it was used to produce 42 per cent of all electricity in 2003.

OIL

Europe, with the exception of the UK, Norway and Russia, has few oil deposits. So Europe is a big consumer of oil, using 19.6 million barrels per day out of a world total of 78.1 million barrels. The UK and Norway have oil fields in the North Sea, while Russia has large oil fields in Siberia. Oil from Russia is sent by pipeline to the countries of western Europe, especially France, Germany and Spain. Russia produces 8.5 million barrels of oil per day and sends 4.9 million barrels per day to the rest of Europe. The Middle East sends Europe 3.2 million barrels of oil per day (27 per cent of the total) and another 1.8 million barrels per day are sent from North Africa. Oil is also sent to Europe from Africa and South America.

A North Sea oil rig. In 2003, the estimated North Sea reserves amounted to 15,900 million barrels. If production continues at the present rate, North Sea oil will run out some time between 2009 and 2013.

NUCLEAR POWER

Nuclear power stations are important throughout Europe. They have the advantage of being non-polluting, provided they are safely managed. However, they are also expensive to build, and difficult to close down. If radioactive waste is not stored correctly underground, radioactive substances may escape into the air or the water table. And if the waste is stored above ground, the storage facilities have to be strong enough to withstand natural disasters and/or terrorist attack. Any leakage of radioactive material can lead to severe sickness or death in animals and people.

In 1986 there was a serious accident at Chernobyl, a nuclear power station in the Ukraine, and radioactivity escaped into the atmosphere. Some places in the area are still uninhabited, and many children have been born with defects. The cloud of radioactivity from the power station spread over much of western Europe and rainfall washed radioactive particles into the soil. Even in 2004 the soil was still so badly contaminated in affected areas, such as North Wales, that meat from sheep raised there could not be sold for human consumption.

RENEWABLE ENERGY SOURCES

Renewable energy sources are sources that will not run out. They include hydro-electric power (HEP), wave/tidal power, wind power, solar power, geothermal energy, and biomass fuels such as wood (provided they are replenished faster than they are consumed).

A hydro-electric power station in Romania. In 2002, HEP provided 31.2 per cent of Romania's electricity.

Hydro-electric power (HEP) is important in countries like Austria and Switzerland, which have no oil or coal. A dam is built across a river valley to store water, which can then be channelled through turbines in the dam wall to generate electricity. Russia and Romania have large HEP facilities and many other European countries, including France and the UK, make use of HEP.

Tidal waters in coastal areas or river estuaries can also be used to generate electricity by channelling the waters through turbines. Tidal power is being used on the River Rance in France to generate electricity. In Norway special turbines have enabled engineers to capture the power of the waves in a similar way, and wave power is also now in commercial operation in Scottish waters.

Geothermal energy utilizes the natural heat in the Earth's crust. For instance, in Iceland bore-holes tap hot water underground which is used to heat homes and offices. Steam from underground is also used in power stations in Italy and Iceland, where it drives turbines to generate electricity.

• • • • • • ▷ IN FOCUS: Wind power

Wind turbines capture the energy of the wind using rotor blades, which transfer this energy to a motor that generates electricity. Wind turbines have been built in many European countries including Denmark, Spain and the UK, and are often clustered in large numbers to make a wind farm. In the UK, the goal is to produce 10 per cent of the country's electricity from renewable sources, such as wind, by 2010. By 2005 there were 93 wind farms in the UK, producing enough electricity to power 495,000 homes and saving 2 million tonnes (1.9 million tons) of carbon dioxide emissions. However, wind farms have been criticized for the noise they create, the bird deaths they cause and their visual intrusion.

A wind farm in Andalucia, Spain.

Eucalyptus trees being grown in central Portugal for the paper-making industry.

Some houses in Europe have solar panels on their roofs, which capture the heat of the sun and use it to heat domestic water systems. Photovoltaic (PV) cells can also be mounted in solar panels to convert the energy of the sun into electricity, but PV technology remains expensive and is not widely used at present.

OTHER RESOURCES

Although some of Europe's forests have been cut down, forest industries are still important in parts of Russia, Poland, Germany, Portugal, Spain, Sweden, Wales and Scotland. For instance, in central Portugal, fast-growing eucalyptus trees have been planted in the Alentejo region in order to provide wood pulp for the local paper-making industry.

Until the early twentieth century, Europe's coastal waters were only used for small-scale fishing and sailing. Since then, they have been utilized in other ways, including underwater mining, industrial and domestic waste disposal, tourism and conservation. Some of these uses conflict with each other so management schemes have been introduced. For example, the dumping of industrial waste in the North Sea is controlled by an agreement between all the countries with a North Sea coastline.

Fishing is still important in Europe, especially in Iceland and Spain. However, the switch from local fishing fleets to huge ocean trawlers has led to many years of overfishing, leaving fish stocks dangerously low. In most of Europe, restrictions on catches have been imposed, in the hope that stocks of cod and

herring will recover. In some places, such as the west coast of Scotland, fish farms have been established to raise salmon and other fish in large cages set within the sea lochs (narrow coastal inlets, protected from the open sea).

Fish farms, such as this salmon farm in Scotland, account for an increasing proportion of the fish consumed in European countries.

The Mediterranean and other European seas have been used for the disposal of industrial and domestic waste for over 80 years but attempts are now being made to clean them up. In recent years, large quantities of agricultural chemicals, such as fertilizers and pesticides, have run into these seas, causing the rapid growth of algae. In the Adriatic Sea, the algal blooms can be up to 10 metres (30 feet) deep and 10 km (6 miles) wide. The algae kills fish, pollutes beaches and causes disease in the people and animals that bathe in it.

FACT FILE

In 2004, Europe's fish farms were producing about 10 million tonnes (9.8 million tons) of fish each year.

Europe used to be rich in iron, copper, zinc and nickel. However, many of these deposits have been exhausted so Europe has become a big importer of minerals. Russia has large deposits of lead, zinc, silver and nickel as well as copper and even gold, especially in Siberia. Although the harsh Siberian climate makes extraction of these minerals difficult and expensive, more of them are being shipped to the EU as demand continues to grow.

6. THE EUROPEAN ECONOMY

When the European Economic Community (EEC) was established in 1957, it became the world's second-largest economy (after the United States). It has grown in importance as its membership has expanded to the present 25 members of the renamed European Union (EU). In 2003, for example, the EU countries (then just 15 members) accounted for half of all international commerce. The EU's economic success was aided by the creation of a large single European market in 1993, which stimulated economic growth within EU countries. A common currency, the euro, was introduced in 1999 and by 2001 had led to a further 10 per cent increase in intra-European trade. In January 2002, the euro formally replaced national currencies in 12 of the member countries.

Euro notes and coins.

ECONOMIC GROWTH AND UNEQUAL SHARES

The addition of ten new EU members (Latvia, Lithuania, Estonia, Hungary, Poland, Slovakia, Slovenia, Malta, Cyprus and the Czech Republic) in May 2004, and the expectation that more EU members will adopt the euro as their national currency, is likely to boost the EU's economic growth even further in future. Several of the new member countries have extensive raw materials, such as iron ore in Latvia, and timber, sulphur and coal in Poland. Oil and gas from Russia and coal from Poland will also help to fuel European economic development in the twenty-first century.

However, economic growth is not occurring evenly across Europe. The richer, industrial countries, such as Germany, the UK, Denmark and Sweden, are developing at a faster rate

People in Europe are increasingly concerned about their quality of life (the well-being of their community and the area in which they live). Quality of life is based on several factors, including housing conditions, life expectancy and environmental pollution. Most of these factors depend on government spending on sectors such as health, education, transportation and the environment. But social expenditure of this kind varies from country to country. In Sweden and Norway, for example, government spending on healthcare in 2002 was equivalent to 7 per cent of GDP, whereas in Latvia and Moldova it was equivalent to just 3 per cent of GDP. The United Nations monitors quality of life around the world and in 2002 ranked Norway, Sweden, the Netherlands, Belgium and Ireland within the top ten countries. By contrast, Romania, Ukraine and Turkey were ranked the lowest of the European countries, below countries such as Mexico, Libya and Argentina.

than the poorer ones, such as Moldova, Romania and Belarus in eastern Europe. For example, the average income in Romania in 2003 was just US$2,310 (compared to US$33,750 in Denmark).

The EU is trying to reduce inequalities between people living in different member countries by helping poorer regions develop their economies. For example, companies may be given money to encourage them to build new factories in areas where old industries have closed down and unemployment is especially high. The EU also provides money to help establish new businesses, and gives grants for improving infrastructure (such as roads and bridges) that may encourage businesses

A shopping centre in Birmingham, UK. Thanks to rising wages and lower unemployment, people in the UK now have around 15 per cent more disposable income, than they did in the mid-1980s.

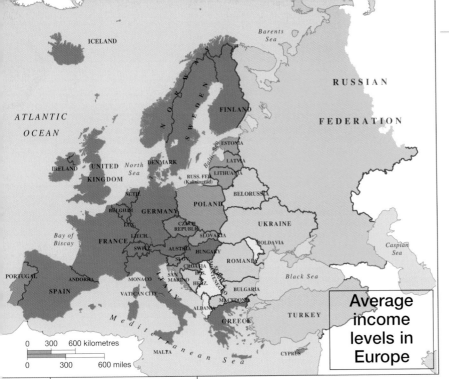

Average income levels in Europe

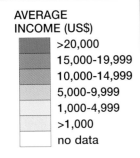

AVERAGE
INCOME (US$)

- >20,000
- 15,000-19,999
- 10,000-14,999
- 5,000-9,999
- 1,000-4,999
- >1,000
- no data

A popular beach at Motril, in southern Spain.

to locate there. For instance, many bridges, road improvements and community centres in western Ireland and western Scotland have been paid for by the EU Regional Fund.

SERVICE INDUSTRIES

In Europe, primary industries, such as farming and fishing, have been declining since the early twentieth century. In their place, the manufacturing sector has been growing. The last 50 years have also seen enormous growth in service industries. By 2004, over 60 per cent of all working people in Europe were employed in service industries, from insurance, finance and banking to retail, health, education and tourism.

TOURISM

Tourism is one of the fastest-growing service industries, partly because people generally have more time and money to spend on holidays and day trips. Cheap airline travel and improved motorways have also fuelled this growth.

Southern Italy, Spain, the Greek islands, Portugal and southern France all have many visitors because of their long, hot, dry summers and mild winters. They also have sandy beaches, warm seas and many cultural attractions. Colder countries further north, like Austria, Switzerland, Norway and Romania, attract millions of visitors to their snow-covered mountains for winter sports, including skiing, tobogganing and snowboarding. Meanwhile, northern Italy, Russia, Estonia, the Czech Republic, mainland Greece and the UK offer cultural holidays for those eager to see such historic sights as the Tower of London or the Acropolis in Athens. European cities like Rome, Paris, Berlin, Barcelona, Amsterdam and Prague also attract visitors to their historic buildings, museums and art galleries.

Young tourists pass the Colosseum in Rome.

Europe attracted 400 million visitors (or 57 per cent of all world tourism) in 2002. European tourism also dominated global tourist earnings in 2002, earning US$240 billion (or 51 per cent of the world total). Tourism is clearly a major industry in Europe, with hundreds of thousands of people employed in hotels, restaurants and leisure attractions, as well as selling goods, such as clothing, beachwear and souvenirs.

The tourist industry brings new jobs, better roads and airports, and money to pay for national parks to protect vulnerable, ecologically important areas. However, because tourism is seasonal, there are employment problems out of season. Tourism can also create competition for the best land, forcing prices up until locals can no longer afford to buy property. In particularly popular destinations, such as the island of Crete or the Spanish coast, tourism may lead to overcrowding,

FACT FILE

Demand for skiing in the French Alps is so great that new complexes have been built as high as 1,800 m (5,905 feet) and 2,000 m (6,560 feet) above sea level. However, some of these new buildings are in areas that are prone to avalanches.

FACT FILE

Equipment used to monitor environmental pollution has become big business in Germany. In 2003, Germany produced around 20 per cent of the world's environmental monitoring equipment.

A highly automated plant producing BMW cars in Regensburg, Germany.

insensitive development and pollution, eventually damaging the beaches that attracted visitors to begin with.

INDUSTRY IN EASTERN EUROPE

Industry in much of eastern Europe, including Russia, the Baltic republics, Moldova, Romania and Ukraine, was controlled by communist central planning from 1917 until 1991. Since the fall of communism in eastern Europe, there have been drastic changes. Old, inefficient machinery has been updated in steel, chemical and engineering plants, transforming cities like Krakow (in Poland) and Dresden (in former East Germany) into modern industrial centres. This type of modernization can be difficult and expensive, and has sometimes led to increased unemployment and a temporary reduction in living standards. Change has been more gradual in Hungary and the Czech Republic, where there have been fewer mass redundancies and a less dramatic decline in female employment.

INDUSTRY IN WESTERN EUROPE

In western Europe heavy industries, like steel, chemicals and engineering, have declined since the 1980s because of competition from cheaper producers in China, South Korea and eastern Europe. As a result, some old industrial areas, such as the Black Country in central England and the Massif Central in south central France, have lost both industries and population. Others, like the Ruhr in north-western Germany, have been able to adapt and develop new industries, such as making washing machines, DVD players and televisions.

Sometimes new industries, like computer and electronic equipment manufacturing, have developed in areas with no previous industries, as in Estonia, southern Bavaria in Germany, and the 'M4 corridor' (a line of towns, including Reading and Maidenhead, along the M4 motorway in southern England). Today, many of Europe's key industrial areas are located close to transport links (ports or motorways) or large centres of population such as Stuttgart in south-western Germany. This relocation of industry has taken place because proximity and access to markets has become more important than being located close to raw materials or power sources, as was the case in the past.

Many European industries are today owned by powerful transnational companies (TNCs), whose headquarters may be located in a different country, or even continent. Such companies typically assemble products, such as cars, or manufacture equipment, including computers or mobile phones. Parts are imported from all over the world and the product is then assembled in Spain or France or the UK. Some Japanese companies, such as Toyota and Nissan, have invested in factories in the UK to take advantage of the UK's skilled labour force and access to the EU market. However, in future, many of these companies are likely to assemble their goods in eastern European countries because labour costs are lower there.

FARMING

Most farming in western Europe incorporates modern technology and the use of chemicals to get the maximum yield from crops and livestock. Maize, sugar beet and wheat are important crops, together with fruits and vegetables, such as strawberries, lettuce and tomatoes. In Mediterranean countries like

FACT FILE

There are still a few places in Europe where there are few or no taxes, such as the Regio Basilensis area around Basle in Switzerland. Companies are keen to relocate to these places in order to reduce their tax bills.

This woman receives relatively low wages for her work at a shoe factory in Borovo, Croatia. Many companies are eager to take advantage of low labour costs in countries like Croatia, Estonia and Romania.

Italy and Spain, farmers mainly cultivate tree crops, such as olives and peaches, as well as vineyards and wheat fields. More recently, rice and tobacco have also become popular on the irrigated areas close to Marseilles in France and along the River Rhône. Agricultural produce is sold mainly within Europe. Some agricultural produce is exported and some is sold on the world market after it has been processed into particular high-value products, such as olive oil or cheeses and beverages (especially wine and beer). EU countries produce around 80 per cent of the world's olive oil, for example, and export mainly to the USA, Canada and Australia.

Farming in eastern Europe makes less use of modern machinery and chemicals. In some former communist countries, such as Russia and Romania, farms used to be owned by the state. These farms have now been sold off but the system is still very inefficient. Major investment is needed to bring farming standards up to those of western Europe, especially in terms of technology. For example, over 35 per cent of Russia's milk and dairy produce has become unsaleable by the time it reaches the market because transport is so poor and there is little refrigeration. Horse-drawn ploughs are still widely used in eastern European countries such as Poland because of a shortage of mechanical tractors (but this is changing, now that Poland is a member of the EU).

FACT FILE

In 2003 agriculture employed 23.8 per cent of Portugal's population, while in the more industrialized UK the figure was 2.6 per cent.

A horse-drawn plough in use in Moldova.

THE COMMON AGRICULTURAL POLICY

Economic factors are becoming increasingly important in European farming. The Common Agricultural Policy (CAP) was established by the EEC (now EU) in 1962, with the aim of protecting farmers' incomes and increasing food production, and thereby reducing the need for imports. The CAP sets minimum prices for farm products so farmers know they will be able to make a profit. The CAP also offers farmers grants to buy new machinery or to help them switch to new crops such as avocados and kiwi fruit, as in areas near Barcelona, Spain, and Faro, Portugal.

The CAP has achieved many successes, including increased food production. For example, the average European wheat yield grew from 4.4 tonnes (4.3 tons) per hectare in 1970 to 6.5 tonnes (6.4 tons) per hectare in 2002. The CAP has also helped farmers working in difficult areas by giving them grants and low-interest loans. However, there has been much criticism of the CAP because it takes up 70 per cent of the entire EU budget. The CAP has also created surpluses of some foods, such as grain, milk and wine. In addition, the environment has suffered from the use of too many agrochemicals, which have poisoned wildlife.

FACT FILE

Intensive plasti-culture (hothouse farming using long tunnels made from plastic) is the most profitable type of agriculture in Spain. However, it uses large quantities of water in a country where water is in short supply, and there have been claims that it involves exploitation of migrant workers.

French farmers block a motorway near Strasbourg, on the French-German border, during a demonstration in September 2000. The farmers were protesting against increases in fuel prices, which almost tripled in 2000.

FOSEA - CCJA
TRUCHTERSHEIM

7. EUROPE IN THE WORLD

MORE GOODS ARE TRADED IN AND OUT OF EUROPE THAN anywhere else in the world. Many European countries import raw materials and semi-manufactured goods, manufacture them into products with more value and then sell them back to the rest of the world. As a result, countries like Germany and the UK have become extremely wealthy. Some people argue that this puts poorer countries in the developing world, such as Uganda and Zambia, at a disadvantage, because it makes it harder for them to develop their own industries. Other people argue that, through increased trade, these poorer countries can earn foreign currency.

In 2004, 349 million tonnes (or 343.5 million tons) of goods passed through the port of Rotterdam in the Netherlands.

TRADE AND INDUSTRY

Europe's manufacturers import raw materials from all over the world. For example, European countries import iron ore from Brazil, cocoa from Ghana, cotton from India and oil from Saudi Arabia. However, transnational companies, with their headquarters in Europe, often own the companies that ship the goods, as well as the processing factories and the retail outlets. In some cases they may even own the sites producing the raw materials too. Most of the profit is therefore made in Europe, rather than in the developing countries exporting the raw materials.

Meanwhile, countries that manufacture goods have done quite well in trade with Europe. For instance, Europe imports large

FACT FILE

Around 40,000 multinational companies, of which 13,000 are European, dominate two-thirds of world trade.

quantities of electronic parts and electronic goods from Japan and other East Asian countries, such as South Korea and China. Textiles, clothing and footwear come to Europe from China, India and Taiwan. In some of these countries, lower labour costs and fewer environmental regulations mean that goods can be produced more cheaply than in Europe.

Exports from Europe are mostly manufactured goods, especially machinery, transport equipment and chemicals. Most exports go to other European countries or to the United States and Japan. Trade can also dramatically expand or reduce employment opportunities. Between 1980 and 2003, exports of goods from the 12 countries that share the euro currency and comprise the European Monetary Union (EMU), increased by 294 per cent to US$2,422 billion. Meanwhile, imports into the EMU increased by 223 per cent over the same period to US$2,257 billion. This growth in trade helps determine the success or failure of companies. If a company in one area is not as efficient as another it may be forced to close down. Companies will make things wherever manufacturing costs are lowest, and this increases employment opportunities in countries with lower labour costs, such as Portugal and Romania, where a large number of German electronic products are now made.

AID AND PEACEKEEPING

Europe gives a lot of aid, which in 2003 amounted to $US7.2 million (the USA gave $US16.2 million) to poorer countries. Aid takes many forms, from food, tents, medicines and water purification equipment supplied after disasters such as earthquakes, floods and droughts, to longer-term financial aid, designed to help the country as a whole. This might involve giving

A healthcare worker from a French aid agency in action in Africa.

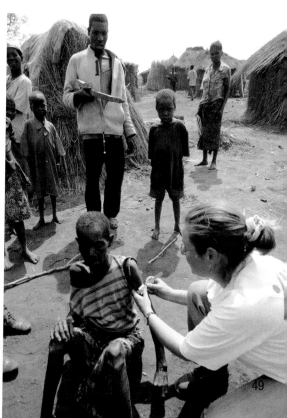

49

money for new farming equipment or new factory machinery. Some aid is in the form of doctors, nurses, scientific advisers or teachers who go to work on government-sponsored programmes in poorer countries. Some of the aid is sent directly from one nation to another, and this is called bilateral aid, and some is sent via the United Nations or the EU and is called multilateral aid. Many non-governmental aid organizations are based in Europe. These include Oxfam, Christian Aid and Action Aid.

European countries have also provided military and peacekeeping forces to be used in countries where there is conflict. For example, in 2000 troops from the UK, France, Italy, Russia and Spain were sent to the former Yugoslavia to help keep the peace between different ethnic groups. More recently, troops from the UK, Spain and Italy were sent to Iraq to fight alongside US troops in the war in that country, and some remain there on peacekeeping duties after the overthrow of Saddam Hussein. Some countries, such as France and Germany, were opposed to the war in Iraq and so did not send troops either before or after the main offensive action.

British troops secure a rooftop position near Basra, in Iraq, in 2003.

Ultimately, the EU hopes to establish a Rapid Response Force, composed of troops from member countries to be sent to any part of the world where there is conflict, but so far the member states have not been able to agree on how this would work. Europe is also using diplomatic efforts to try to resolve disputes within Europe itself. One example is the partition of the island of Cyprus into Greek and Turkish sections, since the Turkish invasion of Cyprus in 1974. Greece and most of Europe have refused to recognize the Turkish part of the island because the invasion was illegal. Now the EU is working to persuade Turkey to recognize diplomatically the Greek part of the island so that Turkey may be allowed to join the European Union.

A UNITED STATES OF EUROPE?

The idea that, as the European Union grows and develops, it may lead to a united Europe has been widely discussed. In theory, Europe could have one common currency, a set of common policies on defence and finance, and one parliament with one set of laws that apply everywhere. However, Europe is a set of different nation states, each with their own ideas

A meeting of the EU held when 10 new members joined the European Union in May 2004.

and traditions. Some of these countries are fiercely independent in such matters as defence and finance and would never want to be part of a united Europe.

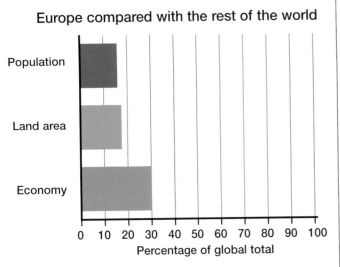

Europe compared with the rest of the world

Population

Land area

Economy

0 10 20 30 40 50 60 70 80 90 100
Percentage of global total

Source: United Nations; World Bank; Britannica Book of the Year 2004

EUROPE AND THE WORLD

Europe has had a lasting influence on the rest of the world in a number of ways. For example, in ancient Athens, as long ago as the fifth century BC, the basic democratic ideas of the law being the highest authority and of citizens being bound by the collective will of the people were established. Since then, democracy has developed into a more sophisticated political system, based on the principles of freedom and accountability, that has spread around the globe.

In August 2003, crowds in Calcutta, India, watch a train pulled by two vintage steam engines during a celebration of the 150th anniversary of Indian Railways.

European colonization has left its legacy in much of the world, such as the use of French and English as national languages in large parts of Africa. Similarly, the railway system in much of India, Pakistan and Bangladesh was designed by the British and built with local labour, and still forms the basis of the railway system of those countries.

Europe's history of colonization also involved a great deal of violence and suffering, including the capture and transporting of millions of people as slaves from Africa to the Caribbean and North America in the seventeenth and eighteenth centuries.

Europe has a long tradition of architecture, which has also influenced many parts of the world. For example, cities in South America, such as Bogota in Colombia and Recife in Brazil, have a central city square with a church or cathedral on one side and public buildings such as the town hall on the other. This pattern of city development is based on that of Spain and Portugal, which colonized these parts of the world in the sixteenth century.

• • • • • • ➤ IN FOCUS: Russia and the world

Because of its size and geographical position, Russia is a special case within Europe. Russia is the largest country in the world and stretches from the shores of the Baltic Sea in the west to the Pacific Ocean in the east. It covers a huge area, about 17 million sq km (6.6 million sq miles), and is rich in natural resources such as oil, gas, timber and minerals. In addition, it has a well-educated population of 143.2 million people. Russia has close links with China, with whom it shares a frontier, as well as other Asian countries such as Japan and South Korea. This means that Russia looks more to Asia than most other European countries do. Russia also has close links with Central Asian countries, such as Kazakhstan and Uzbekistan, which used to be part of the Soviet Union.

The building of the Trans-Siberian Gas Pipeline in Russia in 1983. During construction, tubes were welded and heated to extreme temperatures, before the join was coated with tar.

8. European Wildlife and Conservation

*I*N THE PAST, EUROPE WAS HOME TO A WIDE RANGE OF WILDLIFE, including brown bears, wolves, wild boar, elk and lynx. Over the last hundred years, many of these animals have been hunted to extinction, or their habitat and food supply have been destroyed by human activities, such as the conversion of wild habitats to farmland or urban uses. However, a few still survive. For example, in Spain the Iberian Lynx is the world's most endangered feline. There are about 400 of these animals living in wild woodland areas in southern Spain and about 50 in Portugal. Meanwhile, the number of wolves in Spain has increased from 500 in 1970 to about 2,000 in 2003, as a result of government protection. In Poland, brown bears, wild cats and wolves also survive in the mountainous forests of the south.

These two Iberian Lynx are part of a breeding programme in a Spanish zoo, which is trying to prevent the world's rarest feline from becoming extinct.

Wildlife and National Parks

All European countries are interested in protecting both wildlife and areas of outstanding natural beauty, so that future generations can enjoy them. One way to do this is by designating some areas as national parks. In Europe as a whole, there were 1,687 areas set aside as national parks, nature reserves or wilderness areas by 2003. Together with other protected areas, these made up around 8.5 per cent of

Europe's total land area. Austria, Germany and Switzerland have the largest proportions of protected land (at 36, 32 and 29 per cent respectively), while Russia has the largest area at 1,286,990 sq km (496,907 sq miles).

People enjoying the outdoors in a national park in the Peak District, in the UK.

WASTE AND RECYCLING

Every European household generates an average of 30-75 kg (66-165 lb) of rubbish each month. Much of this rubbish ends up in landfill sites, but these sites are rapidly filling up. Some waste goes to incinerators, where it is burned to generate electricity but this can cause air pollution. However, in many countries, including France, Germany, Austria, the UK and Switzerland, glass, paper and metal are now separated and recycled, with the aim of reducing the rate of tree-felling in Europe's already depleted forests.

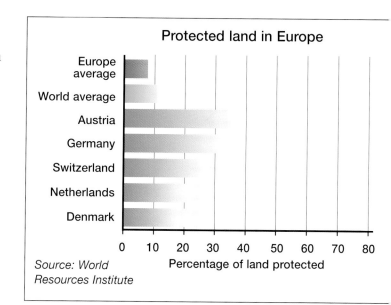

Protected land in Europe

Source: World Resources Institute

Percentage of land protected

POLLUTION PROBLEMS

It takes little to upset the delicate balance between man and nature in Europe's many different environments. For instance, in Spain and Portugal, the construction of new holiday resorts has destroyed large areas of coast and the ecosystems of plants, insects and animals that lived there. In addition, the increased use of artificial fertilizers, pesticides and insecticides on crops throughout Europe has killed wildlife, such as frogs, insects and small mammals such as the shrew, and polluted the water in places like the delta of the River Rhône in France. Factory and power station chimneys all over Europe send thousands of pollutants, such as sulphur dioxide, into the air. These emissions have helped to create acid rain, which has polluted rivers, lakes and streams and killed the fish in them. However, much has been done to reduce air pollution from factories, and many rivers, like the Rhine in Germany and the Thames in London, are now clean enough for fish and otters to live in them again.

Some industrial concerns have been reluctant to change their practices because of the cost. For example, it cost £4 billion to fit pollution control equipment to all coal-burning power stations in the UK between 1995 and 2001. Yet a great deal of British pollution ends up in Scandinavia or other parts of Europe and there is debate as to who should pay for the clean-up. The EU has been playing an increasingly important role in dealing with the issue of cross-border pollution. For instance, the Environmental Programme for the Mediterranean (EMP), which is cleaning up the Mediterranean Sea, is funded by the EU and by the countries surrounding the Mediterranean.

Pollution in eastern Europe is particularly bad because little was done in the past to protect the environment. For example, some chemical, engineering and metal

Trees blackened by acid rain in Norway. Damage caused by acid rain costs Norway about US$458,256,305 each year.

works and oil refineries in Hungary, Romania and Bulgaria pour their waste products into the River Danube, and the river now contains many life-threatening contaminants, from mercury and cadmium to nuclear waste.

WISE STEWARDSHIP FOR THE FUTURE

In Sweden, people are trying to reduce energy consumption and pollution. For example, Hammarby Sjostad, in Stockholm, Sweden's capital, used to be an industrial dockland area, but in 1999 the Swedish government began redeveloping it to minimize the impact on the environment. So, for instance, waste water is recovered from the sewage plant and re-used, and the silt is converted into biogas. Waste from the area is thus recycled as heat, and food waste is composted into the soil.

In addition, public transport by train, boat and trams is easy and fast, which helps to reduce car use. There are clearly marked cycle and pedestrian routes and on-line shopping is encouraged. The 8,000 apartments built by 2004 will have increased to 20,000 apartments by 2012, and they all use low-energy lighting and double-glazing to reduce energy needs. Only if much of Europe is prepared to make these sorts of changes can the environmental damage of the last several hundred years be significantly slowed down or even halted.

The buildings of Hammarby Sjostad are very energy-efficient, using a large amount of glass to capture the sun'sl light and warmth.

● ● ● ● ● ● ➤ **IN FOCUS: Creating green spaces in cities**

Some European cities have created green spaces in order to improve their inhabitants' quality of life. In Germany in the 1980s, for example, the cities of Essen and Bochum used the space created by the decline of old industries such as coal mining and steel making to plant areas with trees. In this way, birds and insects were encouraged back into parts of cities from which they had been absent for years. The open spaces also provide recreation opportunities, including running and cycling tracks, for city-dwellers. In Moscow, green spaces, which were created in the 1950s as the city expanded, have been landscaped to provide Muscovites with places where they can ski in winter and run, stroll or cycle in summer.

9. THE FUTURE OF EUROPE

*E*UROPE FACES A NUMBER OF SERIOUS CHALLENGES IN THE FUTURE. One of these is the gap between rich and poor countries and, within each country, the gap between rich and poor people. The gap between rich and poor countries is being actively reduced by the EU, which works to reduce such gaps by means of its Regional Fund and its Common Agricultural Policy, which both channel funds into poorer nations. Unless these economic inequalities are reduced, resentment of those who migrate from poorer areas in eastern Europe to richer areas in western Europe, in search of better employment opportunities and an improved lifestyle, may continue to cause social tensions.

These Romanian agricultural workers have come to Italy in search of employment.

There are also problems involving potential new EU members, such as Turkey, which has a poor record on human rights. Some politicians argue that such regimes should never be admitted, while others say that joining the EU would help these states to adopt a fairer, more democratic style of government. Often, when considering new applicants for the EU, a country's record on human rights is taken into account as well as its economic situation. As more countries become members, the decision-making process within the EU (which is already very

In October 2004, Turkey's bid to join the EU was backed by the European Greens, a Europe-wide political party that emphasizes the protection of the environment and the peaceful resolution of conflict.

Turkey in the EU: a common future

cumbersome) may become even more time-consuming and lead to damaging delays in implementing important decisions.

THE TERRORIST THREAT

Finally, security will continue to be a major factor in Europe. There were terrorist attacks in Europe before the attack on the USA on 11 September 2001, but they were mostly small-scale bombings carried out by local groups such as the Basque separatists in Spain. However, terrorism has grown as a threat in Europe since 2001, with attacks such as that on a train in Spain in 2003 and on a school in Russia in 2004. All European countries are now co-operating to counter these terrorist threats and members of terrorist groups such as Al-Qaeda have been arrested in Germany and the UK. The level of security is constantly under review and increases as each new threat is uncovered. However, terrorist attacks remain relatively rare in Europe.

French security police patrol Roissy Airport, north of Paris, on Christmas day 2003, after receiving intelligence reports of a planned terrorist hijack attack.

STATISTICAL COMPENDIUM

Sources: UN Agencies, World Bank and Britannica

Nation	Area (sq km)	Population (2003)	Urbanization (% population) 2003	Life expectancy at birth 2002 (in years)	GDP per capita (US$) 2002	Percentage of population under 15 years 2003	Percentage of population over 65 years 2003
Albania	28,748	3,166,000	43.8	73.6	4,830	27	7
Andorra	468	71,000	91.7	N/a	N/a	N/a	N/a
Austria	83,859	8,116,000	65.8	78.5	29,220	16	16
Belarus	207,595	9,895,000	70.9	69.9	5,520	17	14
Belgium	30,528	10,318,000	97.2	78.7	27,570	17	17
Bosnia and Herzegovina	51,129	4,161,000	44.3	74.0	5,970	17	11
Bulgaria	110,994	7,897,000	69.8	70.9	7,130	15	17
Croatia	56,610	4,428,000	59.0	74.1	10,240	16	16
Cyprus	9,251	802,000	69.2	78.2	18,360	22	12
Czech Republic	78,866	10,236,000	74.3	75.3	15,780	15	14
Denmark	43,094	5,364,000	85.3	76.6	30,940	19	15
Estonia	45,227	1,323,000	69.4	71.6	12,260	16	15
Faroe Islands	1,399	47,000	38.8	N/a	N/a	N/a	N/a
Finland	338,145	5,207,000	60.9	77.9	26,190	18	15
France	543,965	60,144,000	76.3	78.9	26,920	19	16
Germany	357,002	82,476,000	88.1	78.2	27,100	15	17
Gibraltar	5.8	27,000	100.0	N/a	N/a	N/a	N/a
Greece	131,957	10,976,000	60.8	78.2	18,720	15	19
Hungary	93,030	9,877,000	65.1	71.7	13,400	16	15
Iceland	102,819	290,000	92.8	79.7	29,750	22	12
Ireland	70,285	3,956,000	59.9	76.9	36,360	21	11
Isle of Man	572	75,000	51.8	N/a	N/a	N/a	N/a
Italy	301,323	57,423,000	67.4	78.7	26,430	14	19
Latvia	64,610	2,307,000	66.2	70.9	9,210	15	16
Liechtenstein	160	34,000	21.6	N/a	N/a	N/a	N/a
Lithuania	65,301	3,444,000	66.7	72.5	10,320	18	14
Luxembourg	2,586	453,000	91.9	78.3	61,190	19	15
Macedonia	25,713	2,056,000	59.5	73.5	6,470	22	11
Malta	316	394,000	91.7	78.3	17,640	19	13
Moldova	33,700	4,267,000	46.0	68.8	1,470	20	11
Monaco	1.95	34,000	100.0	N/a	N/a	N/a	N/a
Netherlands, The	41,526	16,149,000	65.8	78.3	29,100	18	14
Norway	323,758	4,533,000	78.6	78.9	36,600	20	15
Poland	312,685	38,587,000	61.9	73.8	10,560	18	13
Portugal	92,135	10,062,000	54.6	76.1	18,280	17	15
Romania	237,500	22,334,000	54.5	70.5	6,560	17	14

Russia	17,075,400	143,246,000	73.3	66.7	8,230	16	13
Serbia and Montenegro	102,173	10,527,000	52.0	73.0	2,200	26	18
Slovakia	49,036	5,402,000	57.4	73.6	12,840	18	11
Slovenia	20,273	1,984,000	50.8	76.2	18,540	15	15
Spain	505,990	41,060,000	76.5	79.2	21,460	15	17
Sweden	449,964	8,876,000	83.4	80.0	26,050	17	17
Switzerland	41,285	7,169,000	67.5	79.1	30,010	16	16
Turkey	779,452	71,325,000	66.3	70.4	6,390	28	6
Ukraine	603,700	48,523,000	67.2	69.5	4,870	16	15
United Kingdom	244,110	59,251,000	89.1	78.1	26,150	18	16

GLOSSARY

Asylum seeker A refugee who claims the right to live in safety in another country.

Baltic states Estonia, Latvia and Lithuania.

Basque country A region in northern Spain.

Capitalism An economic system in which most property is privately owned.

Cold War The hostile relationship between the NATO alliance and the countries allied to the Soviet Union between 1949 and 1990.

Common Agricultural Policy (CAP) The agricultural policy of the European Union from 1962.

Communism A political doctrine based on the communal ownership of property.

Deforestation The removal of trees, shrubs and forest vegetation.

Drought A long period without rainfall.

Dyke Earth wall built to protect land from flooding.

Ecosystem The contents of an environment, including all the plants and animals that live there.

Euzkadi to Askatasuna (ETA) A terrorist group in Spain whose name means 'Basque Fatherland and Liberty'.

Fascism A political movement based on unquestioning obedience to an authoritarian leader.

Geothermal energy Energy extracted in the form of heat from the Earth's crust.

Glacier A large body of ice that moves slowly down a slope or valley or spreads outwards.

Hunter-gatherer Member of a group that lives by hunting animals and gathering wild plants.

Hydro-electric power (HEP) A type of energy generated by fast-flowing water moving through turbines.

Immigrant A person who leaves one country and comes to live in another.

Infrastructure Networks, e.g. railways and phone lines, that allow communication and/or help people and the economy to function.

Intensive farming A type of farming designed to increase the quantity of produce that can be grown on a given area of land, often involving the use of expensive machinery and chemicals.

Irrigation The artificial watering of land to help crops grow.

Marshall Plan Plan by which the USA gave assistance and financial aid to the countries of western Europe, to help them recover from the Second World War.

National park A large, mainly rural area, with outstanding natural scenery and wildlife, that is protected for public enjoyment.

The North Atlantic Treaty Organization (NATO) A defensive military alliance, established in 1949, that includes the USA, Canada and many European countries.

Photovoltaic cell A device in a solar panel that converts the sun's energy into electricity.

Population density Number of people living in a given area in a country.

Protestantism A form of Christianity that originated in the sixteenth century, which denies the authority of the Pope in Rome.

Refugee A person who leaves a country due to persecution for reasons of race, religion, nationality, social group or political opinion.

Renaissance A revival of learning, science and culture in fifteenth-century Europe, based on the works of the ancient Greeks and Romans.

Roman Catholicism The Christian faith and doctrine of the Roman Catholic Church.

Soviet Union Former federation of 15 republics (including e.g. Russia, Estonia, Latvia and Lithuania), formed in 1922, after the Russian Revolution, and dismantled in 1991.

Transnational company (TNC) A very large company with branches in many countries, often with headquarters in Europe or the USA.

Warsaw Pact An alliance of eastern European countries (including the Soviet Union), formed in 1955 and dissolved in 1991.

FURTHER INFORMATION

BOOKS TO READ:

Africa, Europe and Asia: Old World Continents, Brian McClish (Heinemann, 2004)

A Young Citizen's Guide to The European Union, Richard Tames (Hodder Wayland, 2005)

Britannica Learning Library: Views of Europe (Encyclopaedia Britannica (UK) Limited, 2004)

Changing Face of series: *France; Germany; Greece; Ireland; Italy; Poland; Spain; Sweden; United Kingdom* (Hodder Wayland, 2002-2005)

Continents in Close-up: Europe, Keith Lye (Cherry Tree Books, 2001)

Earth's Continents, Brian McClish (Heinemann, 2004)

Immigrants from Eastern Europe, Sarah Horrell (Franklin Watts, 2002)

New Geographies: Europe, Philip A. Sauvain (Nelson Thorne, 2004)

USEFUL WEBSITES:

http://en.wikipedia.org/wiki/Europe
Wikipedia's entry on Europe, including lots of information on the continent and its different regions, and links to Europe-related topics.

www.eurunion.org/infores/teaching/Young/fun.htm
Information and activities about the European Union.

www.lonelyplanet.com/destinations/loc-eur.htm
Online guide to numerous European countries includes facts and figures, culture, history, and tourist information.

www.friendsofeurope.org/
A non-biased organization that promotes discussion and research on the issues surrounding Europe and its future.

http://europa.eu.int/youth/index_en.html
The European Youth Portal from the official EU website.

http://www.ordnancesurvey.co.uk/oswebsite/freefun/games.html
Test your knowledge of European flags or play the Europe jigsaw game from Ordnance Survey.

INDEX

Page numbers in **bold** indicate pictures:

ABOUT THE AUTHOR

David Flint is Head of Primary Teacher Training at University College, Worcester, UK. He has written many educational books for children, including *Curriculum Focus: The Local Area* and *Curriculum Focus: Islands and Seaside* (Hopscotch Publishers).